PRAISE FOR THE AUTHOR(S), THE ARTIST, AND/OR THE BOOK

"…superb, incredible, beautiful!"
– Ray Bradbury, celebrated author of Fahrenheit 451 (quote refers to past art and illustrations by Dixon)

"…Stunning illustration, solid information and the clever juxtaposition of a personal story and sharp marketing advice… the treasure map to creative satisfaction and business success."
– Rebecca Forster, USA Today bestselling novelist

"…Deeply charming and incredibly useful, a perfect metaphor and guide for the writer or artist to the "bridge" between creation and reaching your audience."
– Leslie Daniels, author of the critically acclaimed novel Cleaning Nabokov's House

"…Wow! Crossing the Troll Bridge somehow captures everything that I've learned (by accident) over the past 15 years. The biggest thing to take away? The part about facing fear. All of the points are extremely important and must be followed for a creative person to succeed."
–Eric Joyner, artist at www.ericjoyner.com

"Crossing the Troll Bridge is the how-to guide for navigating the go-to-market process for creative folks."
–C J Meenan, Founder and CEO of Open for Business Ventures

ISBN: 978-0-9963849-0-2

CROSSING THE TROLL BRIDGE

A Fun and Fear-less Guide to Connecting You With the Audience You Love!

BY ROBIN BLAKELY AND FRANK ROBERT DIXON

I KEEP MINIMAL RECORDS, AND MY ART STUDIO TENDS TO GET CLUTTERED. TOO OFTEN, MY DRAWING BOARD WHERE I AM SUPPOSED TO DRAW IS COVERED WITH STACKS OF PAPER AND PENCILS AND MARKERS SO I HAVE TO GO SOMEWHERE ELSE TO DRAW! ONE OF THE CHALLENGES I HAVE HAD IN MY LIFE IS USING MY TIME WELL. ONE OF THE THINGS I TELL MY STUDENTS IS THIS:

"I HAVE A THEORY THAT WE ARE ALL LAZY -- JUST SOME OF US HAVE OVERCOME IT BETTER THAN OTHERS". I LAUGH ABOUT SUFFERING FROM A NOT-SO-RARE "DISEASE" THAT I CALL "FLUCTUATING AMBITION." I LOVE IT WHEN I DO FUNCTION WELL AND GET A LOT OF THINGS DONE IN THE DAY. I AM PRETTY COMFORTABLE FOCUSING ON JUST CREATING MY CREATIONS. **I HAVE ALWAYS LOVED TO DRAW AND PAINT... MAKING PICTURES THAT EXPRESS ME AND MY INTERESTS.** I LEARNED A LOT ABOUT CREATING ART MANY YEARS AGO AS AN ILLUSTRATION MAJOR AT ART CENTER COLLEGE OF DESIGN IN PASADENA, CALIFORNIA. I WORKED AT NASA FOR 2½ YEARS AS A GRAPHIC DESIGNER/ILLUSTRATOR. I'VE ILLUSTRATED A HOW-TO-DRAW BOOK CALLED DRAW FANTASY. BUT IN THE LAST DECADE I SEEM TO LIKE BEST CREATING ART FOR ME. I HAVE CREATED 3 BOOKS IN THE LAST 10 YEARS: DRAWING TREETCH AND OTHER FANTASTIC CREATURES, STRUGGLES OF A TREETCH, AND THE ART OF FRANK ROBERT DIXON.

I HAVE ALSO WRITTEN A 200+ PAGE STORY ABOUT A BOY & THE TREETCH (TREE CREATURES). FOR MANY YEARS I HAVE BEEN TEACHING DRAWING AND PAINTING CLASSES AT QUARTZ HILL HIGH SCHOOL AND ANTELOPE VALLEY COLLEGE IN SOUTHERN CALIFORNIA. I HAVE GOTTEN PRETTY GOOD AT TEACHING AND INSPIRING STUDENTS THE SKILLS TO CREATE ART THAT EXPRESSES THEM....ONE OF MY FAVORITE EXPERIENCES IN LIFE HAS BEEN BEING IN THE MIDDLE OF CREATING A WORK OF ART!

Frank

Frank says he is not a very good business person, but I know he has the capacity to be a great business person. Like most artists and writers, Frank simply needs a different kind of business map, one that he can understand and enjoy.

Robin

I LOVE CREATIVE WORK, BUT I HAVE NEVER BEEN COMFORTABLE JUMPING INTO MARKETING, ESPECIALLY USING SOCIAL MEDIA.

FOR A FEW YEARS NOW I HAVE BEEN WISHING I COULD FIND CLEAR STEP-BY-STEP DIRECTIONS THAT WOULD WALK ME, A CREATIVE ARTIST AND WRITER, THROUGH HOW TO MARKET MYSELF. I NEED A WAY THAT I FEEL GOOD ABOUT AND IN CONTROL. I DON'T LIKE FOCUSING ON HYPE OR MONEY MAKING SCHEMES.

I AM ALSO TIRED OF LOSING OPPORTUNITIES. LIKE, ONE YEAR WHEN I HAD A BOOTH IN ARTIST'S ALLEY AT COMICON IN SAN DIEGO, A STRANGER APPROACHED AND SAID: "I WANT TO BE IN YOUR FAN CLUB!" AND I REMEMBER THINKING "THAT'S NICE. BUT I DON'T HAVE A FAN CLUB."

I'M AFRAID OF MAKING MISTAKES. I DON'T FEEL LIKE I KNOW WHAT TO DO WITH FACEBOOK, TWITTER, PINTEREST, INSTAGRAM, LINKED-IN AND ALL THE OTHER FREE PLATFORMS THAT SEEM TO KEEP POPPING UP ON THE INTERNET. AND I ALSO DON'T WANT TO SPEND HOURS AND HOURS EACH DAY TALKING TO PEOPLE ON SOCIAL MEDIA.

SO, UP UNTIL NOW, I HAVEN'T DONE TOO MUCH.

WHEN ROBIN APPROACHED ME ABOUT MAKING THIS BOOK TOGETHER, I SECRETLY DOUBTED THAT MY MARETING PROBLEMS COULD REALLY BE SOLVED, BUT I WAS HOPEFUL.
I SECRETLY THOUGHT THAT THIS MIGHT BE REALLY GOOD FOR ME— BECAUSE MAYBE BY THE END OF THE BOOK I MIGHT REALLY BE MARKETING MYSELF IN A WAY I LIKED AND FELT IN CONTROL OF!
Frank
By the end of this book Frank does find a new way to enjoy and feel in control of his marketing efforts... and so will you.
Robin

The Table of Contents

Chapter 1

The Journey

If you are an Artist, Writer, or an Idea Person, you are in the right place. We're going to show you how to deal with marketing your creative work in a way that invites your imagination to participate.

As creative people ourselves, we know that you have a yearning feeling—a deep wish—to connect with your very own audience of people who appreciate and understand your unique creations at an innermost level.

That longing to connect with kindred spirits often comes with a lonely sense that there is a huge and hazy distance between yourself and the audience you dream about. Even if you know where they are located, these groups of real people sometimes seem impossibly far away. Don't despair. Your audience is out there. You can connect with your fans. We will show you the way.

Let's start with a story about you...

Imagine that you are a creative person who lives in a large amazing Creative Castle. Inside this place, you enjoy creating treasures like drawings, novels, poems, paintings, or whatever creative specialty you do.

You'd love to see your creations being appreciated by fans from all over the world. But, that desire involves marketing—and, up until now, you have never enjoyed marketing.

You wonder what you can do so more fans will visit your Creative Castle...

(Yes, we know you are probably thinking that in real life you do not live in a castle that looks anything like this– but keep reading. You'll discover that imagining yourself this way changes things.)

One day you realize something important.

The road between you and your audience is very hard to navigate. The only way for fans to visit your Creative Castle is to cross a rickety old Troll Bridge. If they make it past the scary troll, they must then find a way to get through your locked Castle gate.

It's no wonder so few people visit you!

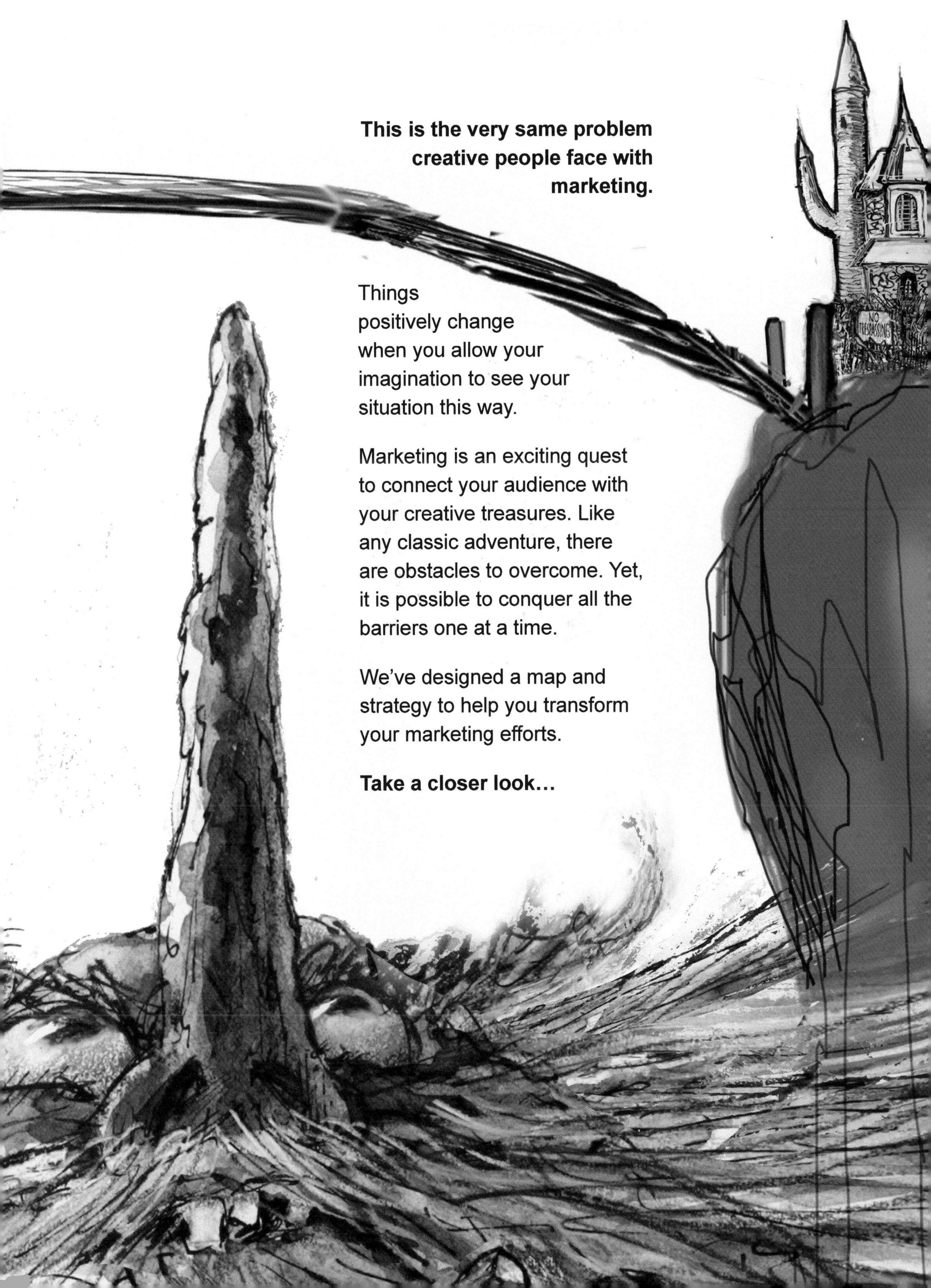

This is the very same problem creative people face with marketing.

Things positively change when you allow your imagination to see your situation this way.

Marketing is an exciting quest to connect your audience with your creative treasures. Like any classic adventure, there are obstacles to overcome. Yet, it is possible to conquer all the barriers one at a time.

We've designed a map and strategy to help you transform your marketing efforts.

Take a closer look…

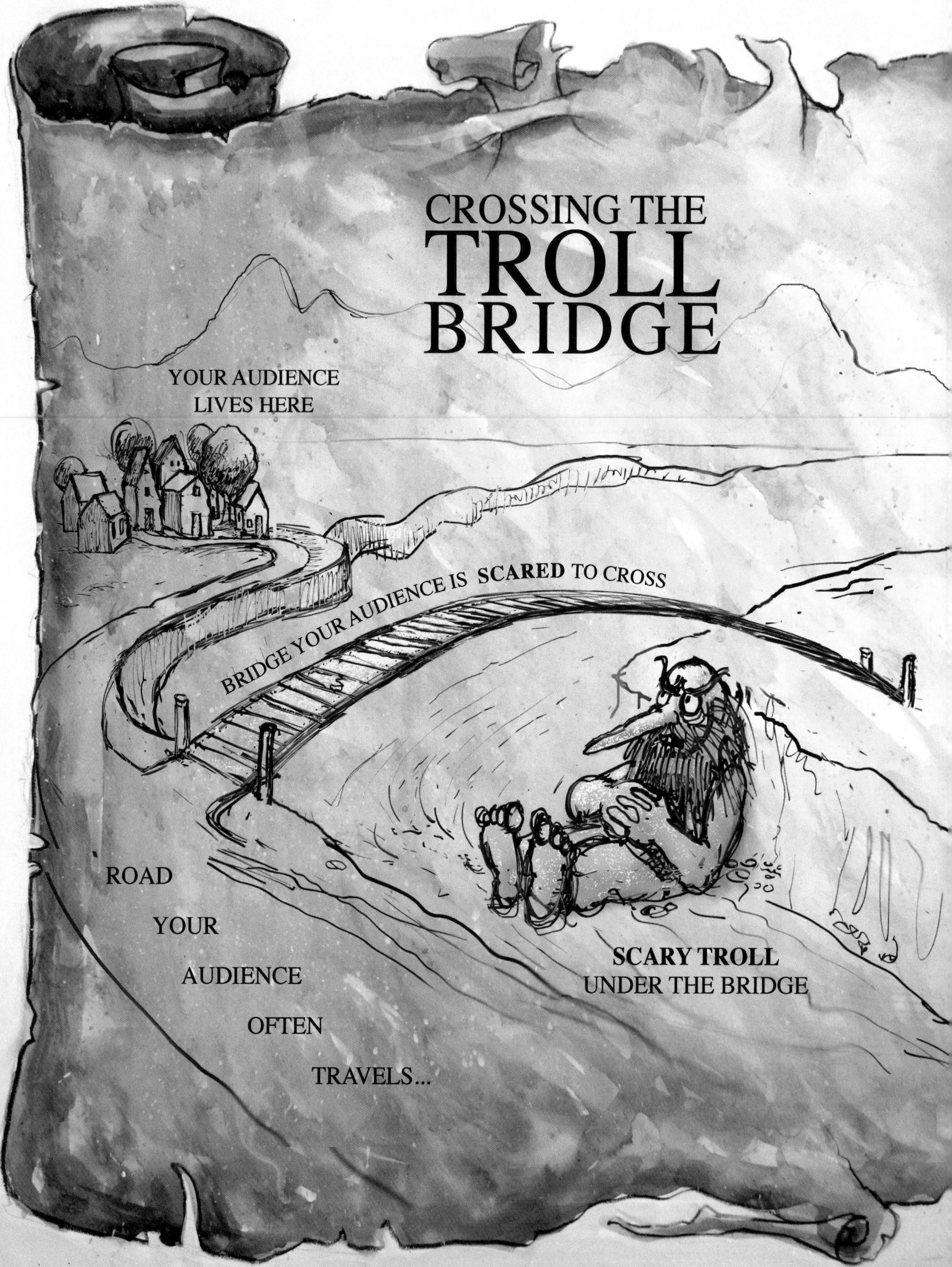

CROSSING THE TROLL BRIDGE

YOUR AUDIENCE
LIVES HERE

BRIDGE YOUR AUDIENCE IS **SCARED** TO CROSS

ROAD
YOUR
AUDIENCE
OFTEN
TRAVELS...

SCARY TROLL
UNDER THE BRIDGE

YOUR CREATIVE CASTLE
(PLACE WHERE YOU LIVE
AND CREATE)
NO
TRESPASSING
NO TRESPASSING SIGN
YOU PUT ON YOUR GATE
FENCE OVERGROWN
WITH VINES AND
BUSHES

Your Quest starts here.

Understanding the inside realm of your Creative Castle will help you build your bridge to the outside world…including conquering that Troll under the bridge. As you become savvy about the purpose of the most important Castle rooms, you will find marketing yourself and your creative work personally and professionally fulfilling.

Come inside and see exactly what we mean.

Chapter 2

The Castle

First of all, the Creative Castle is not a real castle. It is a metaphor for the whole you. You are a creative person who is a unique creative spirit and you are also the creative work you produce, which simultaneously is both separate from you and feels like an extension of yourself.

.

To start, you must clearly understand your identity as a creator. With creative clarity, your marketing strategies will make much more sense and you will be able to make your professional dreams happen—faster.

The Creative Castle represents you, your creativity, your creative space, and the actual physical location where you create. You'll soon see that changing a few small things here can make a big difference in your marketing success.

Many, many rooms exist inside your Creative Castle. Sometimes it can feel hard to understand this vast place and it is common to get lost from time to time as you learn your way around and begin to spend time in each area.

Four rooms are especially critical to your marketing success.

Clearly understanding each of these four areas will help you begin to balance your own priorities, visualize your own boundaries as a creative talent, and ultimately take control of the Troll Bridge.

TO
DREAMERS
TOWER
TO
GRAND
MEETING
ROOM
TO
DOER'S
WORKSHOP

FRANK: What do these castle rooms have to do with marketing?

ROBIN: In real life, the Creative Castle concept is important because traditional approaches to marketing do not embrace the most important needs creative people face when marketing themselves and their work.

FRANK: What needs are overlooked or missing?

ROBIN: Typically, the missing part of the equation is the human side of the issue. Mainly, your marketing concerns as an artist or writer are quite different from the marketing matters surrounding manufactured items like potato chips. The biggest thing to recognize here is that marketing must be handled in a special way for you because you are a different kind of business.

FRANK: Well, yes, of course. I create art. I don't manufacture potato chips.

ROBIN: Yes! So don't allow yourself to be treated like a factory. You are not a machine that turns on and off with a power button. You can't produce items to fulfill orders on demand. You are a human. Because you are a creative individual and you are marketing products and services that you are creating, you must take care of yourself by safeguarding your creative energy, attitude, and emotions.

FRANK: So understanding the rooms inside my Creative Castle will help me understand the human side of marketing?

ROBIN: Yes. This concept will help you discover important strategies that nurture your creativity and therefore enhance your marketing capacity.

Room #1

The Dreamer's Tower

The Dreamer's Tower is where your imagination, passion, and wild ideas are allowed to run free. This room is designed to be a safe place for your talent to incubate and grow. Metaphorically, this is where you go when you dream. It is where you think about ideas for writing a book or drawing a picture or any other creative thing that sparks your imagination. Protecting this creative idea space is important for your growth as an artist or writer. No one should ever be allowed to harshly judge your creative ideas here. No judgmental critics– especially family, friends, or even your own inner critic– are allowed here. This place is where your ideas can be completely free. Hopefully, this place is also a literal space in your real life that you have defined as your office, studio, or creative spot. Literal or figurative, when you recognize and honor that this claimed space is important, your creative work will exponentially become more extraordinary.

Set aside several hours for daydreaming each week. Creative People need time every week to exercise their imaginations. To be productive, feel happy, and stay energized, you need to safeguard your daydreaming time... and use it.

Dream.
Dream.
Dream.

Room #2

The Doer's Workshop

The Doer's Workshop is where you do the things you dream about. This is where you use your skills to bring your ideas to life. This workshop area serves as a sort of combination cook space, exercise room, and scientific laboratory for your skill sets. It is full of all the gadgets and processes and tools that will ultimately create your masterpieces. Your work space will probably have inspiring books and posters, how-to guides, manuals, and all the supplies you use when you create. If you are a visual artist, this place may have paintbrushes, paint, a drawing table or easel, and a computer. If you are a writer, this workshop may have scraps of paper with ideas jotted on them, a laptop, stacks of reference books, and all kinds of other items that you have studied and you want to look at again. This place is all about building up and honing skills. Mentors and coaches may visit you here to offer constructive criticism and advice about polishing your efforts into the finished piece you see in your mind's eye.

Practice. Every writer and artist must master the required levels of craftsmanship for their particular industry—this is the place where, over time and with practice, one's ideas are transformed from undeveloped and amateur creations to finely developed high quality masterpieces.

Practice.
Practice.
Practice.

HOW TO DRAW
PEOPLE
FANTASY
THESAURUS
SKETCHBOOK
DRAW FANTASY
DICTIONARY
HOW TO WRITE A
NOVEL
DICTIONARY

Dreaming and Doing are equally important...

The Dreamer's Tower nurtures creativity.

ROBIN: It's important for people to be able to imagine themselves in their own Creative Castles, but I would like you to show us what it's like for you in your Castle.

FRANK: I could draw a cartoon version of myself in the castle. We could call him "Cartoon Frank".

ROBIN: Good idea! And Cartoon Frank can actually represent any artist or writer, male or female.

Creativity without skill is like an uncut diamond in the rough.

You need both.

The Doer's Workshop nurtures skill.

Skill without creativity is passionless and dull.

The Dreamer's Tower and The Doer's Workshop are critical factors in your success.

Many creative people wonder why they can't garner attention for their work, make a sustainable living, and build a solid lifelong career. It's usually because they have stopped exploring the Creative Castle before they understand the importance of each room.

The truth is before you begin to market yourself and your creative work, you should spend many months and even years enjoying quality time in your Creative Castle's Dreamer's Tower and Doer's Workshop. Never forget that a very human element exists behind all talent-driven products. Writers and artists are not manufacturing factories—we are humans. These two rooms are directly connected to the development, awareness, and well-being of your own talents, dreams, and potential as a creator.

Marketing the creative individual's constantly evolving catalog of creative work is vastly different from marketing manufactured products from a brick and mortar factory. As a human creator, you must take care of yourself in a special way to keep producing creative material. This issue of self-care is relevant to marketing because you are the source for the products and services that will be marketed. If you become overwhelmed or disillusioned, you could simply shut down and put the entire 'company' out of business.

Success requires dreaming and doing. Great ideas are not enough. You must finish your projects.

When you begin to seriously focus on actively marketing yourself and your work, you will need at least one creative treasure that is completely finished.

Here are some Questions that can help you strengthen these two important rooms in your Creative Castle:

- Do you have a designated place that supports your creative endeavors?

- Are there people in your personal or professional world that encourage or even inspire you to use your talents and create? Can you find more encouraging people to have around you? How can you arrange your time and life to be around supportive people more often?

- Are there people in your personal or professional world that criticize or make you doubt yourself? How can you protect yourself from these people? How can you set boundaries around your talent so that your creative gifts are nurtured properly?

- Are you taking time to learn new skills and explore new ideas?

- Are you finishing products and developing services that you can eventually show or sell?

Room #3

The Telescope Tower

This area in the Creative Castle is critical for artists and writers to explore and visit repeatedly across the spectrum of their careers.

The Telescope Tower is where you proactively look out into the world to find and choose your audience. Let's start with the people who will love and appreciate what you do. The concept that you can actually choose your audience is frequently a big turning point for creative people. Taking time to actually seek an appropriate target market is a really big notion. A deliberate approach insists you treat your own work (and yourself) as a treasure worth being found and worth being selectively shared.

The Telescope Tower encourages you to choose your audience, not just take whatever shows up or comes along—like so many creative people unwittingly do, sometimes for their entire careers. It may feel odd at first to take a proactive stance rather than a reactive position. It may feel overwhelming to consider who you want your audience to be. However, everything in your career will change for the better when you put the Telescope Tower to proper use.

It's important to spend sufficient time imagining who your audience could be. Who are the people who will really appreciate your creations? Set aside time to actively consider who these people are. You have many choices and many options. Look into the possibilities. It's okay if you don't know immediately. The telescope tower is about helping you figure it out by exploring.

"Using your telescope" means clearly identifying who your audience is.

As an artist or writer, when you first look through the telescope, the hope is to immediately spot members of your audience. It seems like it should be easy. But sometimes, trying to define your audience is complicated. The effort can be a challenge.

What actually happens may surprise you. You may suddenly feel an overwhelming sense of aloneness. You may quite unexpectedly feel lost or left out. You may feel that the world-at-large is so very far away. It is normal to feel anxious about how far away you seem to be from the rest of the world. It's customary to worry about the barriers or the distance between here and there. It is even possible that you focus on your own troll bridge and feel overwhelmed by its barrier. Don't fret about any of that…not yet. Require yourself to shift the telescope's focus to a different view. Stay on task…Scan the horizon until you find people. From this quiet spot inside your Creative Castle, you can see so many people. Take time to think about who you like and why. You don't have to meet them yet. Just think about who they are. It's important to imagine who you would choose for your audience.

As you consider the great big world full of people, you may stumble over one common idea: "Everybody I lay my eyes on might as well be part of my audience." You may think: "If they don't dislike me, we're good." But this level of acceptance is not good enough. It is not what you and your work deserve. This is an idea you need to rethink. This is an issue that you must manage with great care. You can and need to choose individuals that you sense would love what you do…not just sort-of-like your stuff… not just leak apathy all over you. You deserve people who recognize and celebrate the value of your creative work. Look close. Look hard. The power to make wise choices belongs to you.

Look! Your audience is out there.

Who are the types of folks you would invite to your castle?

The Telescope Tower helps you see beyond your current situation and consider the bigger picture of opportunities.

When you are able to describe your audience in written words, your marketing goals will become clearer (to yourself and to others who can help you connect with your audience).

Here are some Questions that can help you reflect on your audience and find words to identify and describe them:

1. Who likes what you do?
2. Who has ever hired you or bought something you created?
3. Who keeps coming back to look at your work or to ask questions about what you do?
4. Who do you like?

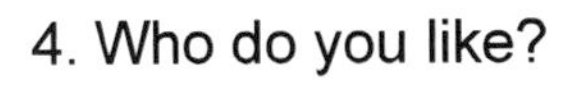

5. Why do you like them?
6. What kind of people are they?
7. What kinds of work do they do?
8. Why do they like what you do?
9. Do they like a certain part of what you do?
10. Do people in your audience share any similarities that would allow us to think of them as groups?
    - Do they come from a certain region?
    - Do they share a certain age range?
    - Do they belong to certain organizations?
    - Do they come from a certain industry or profession?
    - Do they live or work in a certain type of setting like rural, or city, or suburb?
    - Are there more women or more men?
    - Does your work somehow fulfill a common interest or help meet a common goal for these people?

It is important to think about the people who would appreciate your creative treasures. Try to imagine who these people are. You will probably notice that there are just a few types of people that keep coming to mind. Try to narrow it down to four different types of people that will be your audience.

Try to pick four groups. Visualizing your audience as four groups of real people can help you make strong decisions about how to display and showcase your creative work. You can always change your mind. Like any creative work, you must start somewhere. You can choose different groups later. But for now take your best guess and write down four groups.

Room #4

The Grand Meeting Room

As an artist or writer, you must eventually meet your audience. The Grand Meeting Room is an intentional space that can be personally tailored for chosen guests to learn who you are and what you do.

This is a very important concept that will help your imagination bring your brand messaging to life. This is a way to make core marketing strategies more authentic and natural to you. Allowing your imagination to tackle this issue in this way will help you overcome limited thinking you may have developed about marketing yourself and your work.

When you first explore the Grand Meeting Room, it is almost completely empty. Except for four bare tables, the large room is vacant, and it will remain this way until you are completely ready to receive visitors. Utilizing this key area can make your creative career soar to heights you may not have yet imagined, so allow your imagination to work here. The four tables will eventually be used for four very special displays for the four different groups of people who will be your audience. Visualizing your audience as four groups of real people can help you make strong decisions about how to describe your creative work.

Imagine what this room would look like if you carefully arranged each table to delight and intrigue specific guests with displays of your work!

FRANK: I've never considered having my target market come to me. I have typically pictured myself going out to find and interact with my target market on their turf. And since I am not a salesman type of person, I have never done that particularly well.

ROBIN: Well, then, this is the moment when you can turn that idea around in your head. Thinking about your target market in this inbound way is much more natural for artists, writers, and other creative people than the idea of outbound marketing like some kind of door-to-door salesman. This process also helps you define yourself and your work with more power and passion.

The Telescope Tower and The Grand Meeting Room are critical factors in your success.

When you begin to seriously focus on actively marketing yourself and your work, you will need to make sure that you don't lose sight of all the wonderful things marketing can do.

Do not be afraid about money. Making money will happen as a direct result of this meaningful connection.

Enjoy these people.

Enjoy this connection.

Enjoy your time doing creative work.

Always remember: You do not have to choose between enjoyment OR financial compensation...you can have both.

The Telescope Tower and the Grand Meeting Room function in tandem with one another. You need to imagine who your audience is. Then, you must take the next step to imagine what part of what you do will please them. The real key to this important concept is to spend some quiet time considering what you want and who you want to be surrounded by. Then, spend more time actually getting everything ready for the different members of your chosen audience.

Think about ways that you can intentionally make the audience's first visit amazing and memorable. You can– and should– have as much creative fun preparing this destination for your audience, as you do creating one of your best stories or drawings. You also want to be authentic and clear—this will take some time and thought. This Grand Meeting Room effort deserves to have your full attention. Don't rush through it or leave this part to chance.

It's not immediately easy, but you absolutely can do it. It requires some patience and courage, but it is absolutely worth the effort. When you feel confused and alone or stressed and afraid, remember these thoughts:

- You have the right to connect and engage with your audience. Your work can inspire, motivate, entertain, and make a difference to others.

- You deserve to receive the benefits of sharing your amazing creative work with other humans. You deserve to grow creatively as a result of this all-important audience interaction.

Remember that your creative work is your treasure. Share it first with the people who will appreciate its value the most.

Metaphorically, the Creative Castle is really you and your creativity. It's who you are. So, bravely and boldly own every room.

The keys are yours.
The deed is in your name.

Accepting full ownership of your Creative Castle will make a difference in how you live your life in the days, months, and years ahead.

If you do not fully understand what you control, you may wait endlessly for other people to do things that in actuality are clearly in your own sphere of power to make happen. For example, you may believe that if you focus only on producing excellent work that your spot in the world's marketplace will automatically happen...that an audience will magically form for you...that an income stream and a career path will somehow appear. But, usually just creating excellent work isn't enough. You also have to take charge of connecting that work with fans. Understanding the Creative Castle concept can help you understand the entire creative realm with more clarity.

So, grab the keys, take a close look at your castle deed, and then, let's dive into the treasure.

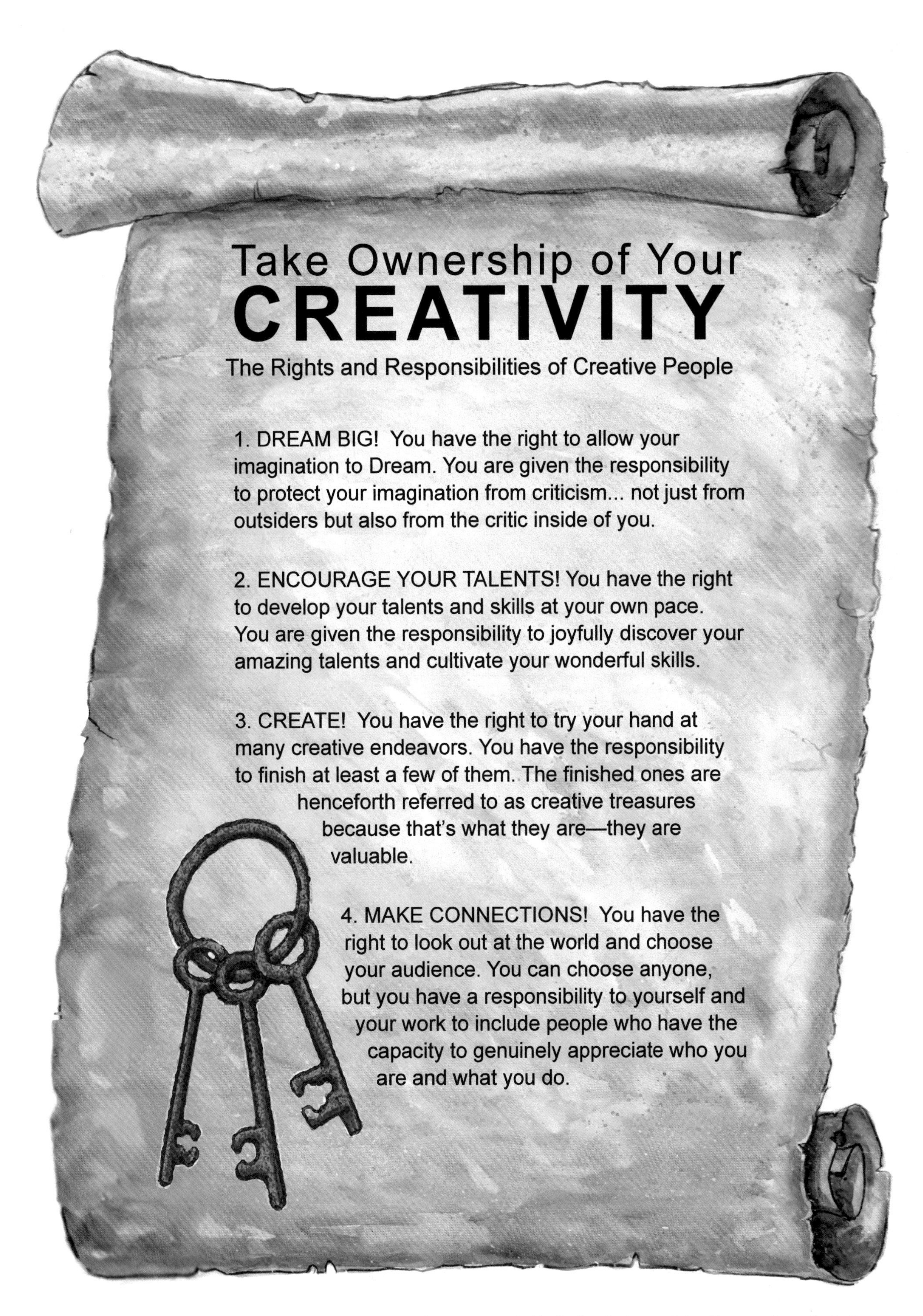

To download your free 8"x10" motivational print of this page (suitable for framing) go to https://gumroad.com/l/uGqE

The Grumpy Old Tree
JASON FLIES HIS KITE
WORDS AND PICTURES BY FRANK ROBERT DIXON

Chapter 3

The Treasure

Your creative work is a real treasure. So it's important that you start treating it with the value it deserves.

Like many artists and writers, you may not have spent much time considering the business side of your creativity—until now. It's very important to make sure that your chosen audience can easily understand who you are and what you do. That means deliberately making your treasures very visible and very tangible so that the audience you choose can experience you and your work without misunderstanding who you are and what you do.

It takes time to get the treasure displayed properly in the Grand Meeting Room. Preparing the displays requires your imagination. Four steps are critical in this process.

Step One: Get All Your Stuff.

It can be hard for many writers and artists to think about sharing their work—deliberately staging the art or the books—so that it can be discovered and enjoyed. Sometimes the very idea feels awkward or pretentious. If it feels weird like that to you, you need to understand something very important:

This isn't about you. This is about helping your audience. It is also about respecting your creative work.

Your audience deserves to connect with your work. The artwork or written words that you produce deserves to be viewed, treated, and cared for as a treasure. Historically, treasure is selectively shared first with people who can appreciate and understand the value of that treasure. That's what we are preparing to do... and it may surprise you how overwhelming this might feel.

The truth is that sharing your creative work can feel scary or exhilarating or both! This is a normal feeling, so don't stop here...keep moving forward.

What do you really need to pull together?

Round up all the creative work you've completed.
Your creative treasures. Your best work.
Your favorite pieces. The ones that define you:

- Everything you've made that you are proud of
- Everything you've done that is great
- Anything that helps showcase your talent and skill
- Anything you want to share with your audience
- Anything that would help make people understand who you are and what you do

For your audience, seeing will be believing. Get started by placing your greatest creative work in a heap. You can sort things out in a bit, but first make sure everything is available and in one place.

Then, what do you do? Simple. Jump in.

After you have gathered your work in one place, you can begin to strategically sort it out.

DRAWING
Treetch
and other
Fantastic
Creatures
By Frank Robert Dixon

The Grumpy Old Tree
JASON FLIES HIS KITE
WORDS AND PICTURES BY FRANK ROBERT DIXON
Draw
MONSTERS
By Frank Robert Dixon

Step Two:
Choose the stuff to go on your first table.

Start with one table. Have one special group in mind. Emphasize the key element that the particular group would be most excited to find out about. Remove any distractions. Help this segment of your audience focus in on what you want them to see most. Personalize the table so that your work shines like a well-set jewel tailored just to them.

ROBIN: Think back to the Telescope Tower. There, you began to focus on four groups. Who did you finally choose?

FRANK: I chose four groups. One is kids who like to draw fantasy creatures; one is artists who want to learn the fantasy art techniques that I teach; one group is museum gallery visitors who love the fine art side of what I do, and one group would be individuals who enjoy one of the special themes in my work—overcoming depression.

ROBIN: Let's pick one of those groups and build a display table that is especially for one specific group. Which one do you pick?

FRANK: Well, that's hard... I guess I'll pick kids who like fantasy creatures as my first one.

Think about how to personalize your first display table for your first audience group:

- Who will this one display table be tailored toward?
- What feelings do you want to help invoke in this particular group of visitors?
- Which of your creative treasures do you want these particular guests to focus on most?
- What should they see first when they come up to the table?
- What colors will be best for this particular display?
- What do you want your visitors to say when they tell their friends about what they have seen?
- What items on this table are available for purchase?
- How can you clearly communicate to your guest the services you provide?

Imagining your work physically displayed on a table helps you rethink and reframe your work so you know how to describe it and share it with real people.

Make an effort to delight and intrigue those future guests by staging your creative treasures in a special way that makes a strong, long-lasting impression.

FRANK: So it looks like this Grand Meeting Room could really help me know more about my target market groups and what they might want to buy.

ROBIN: Yes. Typically, artists and writers can discern at least four different groups of people who appreciate their work. Focusing on preparing your four tables will help make things very clear promotionally. The Grand Meeting Room concept is a solid starting point that can help you imagine real ways to help your target market quickly understand what you do in a way that feels highly personal to them. This effort brings the human element back into the big picture. You want to be able to communicate to people and have them become excited about what you have to offer. This exercise helps your imagination feel free to play and it makes room for your intuition to play a role in the marketing effort as well.

WHEN ROBIN ASKED ME TO CREATE MY DISPLAY TABLES FOR THE ILLUSTRATIONS IN THIS BOOK, SHE SAID:

"MAKE THE TABLE DISPLAYS FEEL LIKE DISNEYLAND!"

THAT HELPED ME A LOT. I STOPPED BEING CONSERVATIVE AND HAD FUN TRYING TO MAKE MY TABLES AS FUN AND APPEALING AS DISNEYLAND. I THINK YOU SHOULD DO THAT TOO WHEN YOU CREATE YOUR TABLES.

TO THE RIGHT IS THE FIRST TABLE I MADE — THE TABLE FOR "CHILDREN WHO LOVE FANTASY ART." AS I THOUGHT ABOUT PRODUCTS TO PUT ON THE TABLE, I REMEMBERED PAST PROJECTS THAT I HAD NEVER FINISHED. ACTUALLY, FOUR OF THE FIVE BOOKS I PUT ON THE TABLE HAVE NOT YET BEEN COMPLETED! (SO NOW I HAVE THE NEW ADVENTURE OF SPENDING THE TIME TO GET ALL THESE BOOKS FINISHED AND PUBLISHED.)

I THOUGHT THE "BIG TREE WITH A SMILING FACE" AND THE FLYING KITTENS WOULD DRAW KIDS TO THE BOOTH. I TRIED TO MAKE IT LOOK FUN AND FESTIVE.

Frank

JASON FLIES HIS KITE
DRAWING
Treetch
Fantastic Creatures
By FRANK ROBERT DIXON
Draw
MONSTERS
By Frank Robert Dixon
THREE BILLY
GOATS GRUFF
LAND OF
Treetch
THE ART OF
FRANK ROBERT DIXON

Step Three:

Focus on the stuff for all four tables (one table at a time).

One at a time, make a table display for the remaining three groups in your audience.

Follow the same steps you took to make the first table. Stay very focused and use your imagination to make each table very distinctly directed to each particular group. If you have a book or piece of artwork that each group will love, include it on each table, but make sure that you focus on the aspect that matters most to the particular group.

FRANK: But how does making these table displays translate to my real life? How will this help me?

ROBIN: I think it is important to literally take a fresh look at your work and see what your audience sees. You will see an item differently when you imagine that you are looking at it from a specific perspective. Your imagination is powerful when you let it do its work. This concept is the right brain's answer to left brain demographics. We need to understand who likes what and why. When we can see the dots connect between your work and your audience, we can apply the info to your promotional tools. You have to start somewhere when you are serious about promotions. This is that starting place. Get your stuff in a big heap and start organizing it with specific audience groups in mind.

FRANK: Do I have to use four tables? What if I want to use three or what if I prefer five?

ROBIN: I believe four is the important number. Somehow progress almost magically happens whenever four tables are used. Maybe it has something to do with patterns or situational dynamics. Maybe it has something to do with how many things people can think about at once. I am not sure why four is the magic number, but I do know it always works best to have four tables. Trying to figure out how to handle four tables may irritate you to some degree. But that irritation is productive in the same way that a grain of sand irritates an oyster...in the end, four tables will mean a pearl is produced. Four is the number that makes that sort of success occur over and over again.

The Art of
FRANK ROBERT DIXON
Draw
MONSTERS
Draw
MONSTERS
DANCING OUT OF THE DUNGEON
SEEKING TO ENJOY THE
ARTIST'S CREATIVE JOURNEY

Step Four:

Think About how the Outside World will view your stuff.

As you design the displays for all four tables, think about the outside world and take some time to reflect on how it feels to you to be seen by them.

Often times, working through the Grand Meeting Room process will help you see yourself with more clarity. You may find that there are better words to use to more effectively describe who you have become as a creator. This new knowledge will become a key to your marketing success. When this information is clear to you, it can be used to articulate you and your work through descriptive phrases on your website and in your promotional materials. This newly found knowledge about your audience can help you determine where to do promotional outreach and where to direct your publicity efforts.

These displays can also ignite your imagination and help you think of future projects that these kindred spirits in your audience might enjoy.

The Grand Meeting Room is often the spot where you and those around you can see your 'brand' emerge or become more clear.

Here are some things to reflect upon:

1. Do these tables help you clearly visualize your audience?

2. Can you imagine additional projects that would be fun to create for these groups?

3. As you produce more work, can you continue to find fun ways to frame your creative work so your target market understands who you are and what you do?

4. Can you imagine great ways to use these tables as points of reference that help shape your promotional messages?

5. As you consider the logistics of what belongs on various tables, you may shed some light on some new ideas.

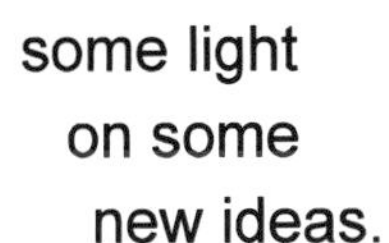

Your audience may not be who you first imagined…that's okay. Additionally, you may get distracted by creative ideas. You may become inspired to do new projects that you never imagined before…that's okay too. No matter what happens, keep working on the four tables until you have completed four displays.

Once the Grand Meeting room is ready, it's time to take on the troll.

Chapter 4

The Troll

The world is filled with many great people who will appreciate your work. Most of these folks would love to visit your Castle to enjoy time with you and your creative treasures. But there's still one big barrier between you and your wonderful audience.
It is the Big Scary Troll!

Every artist and writer must eventually confront and conquer the Troll to succeed at marketing.

We've found that writers and artists become more successful in marketing (and in their own personal life too!) if they take charge of the troll by doing the following three steps.

Step One:

Understand the Troll.

Understanding what that "Troll" is in real life is the key to success.

Metaphorically, the Troll represents all the fears, difficulties, and obstacles that separate you and your fans. In most areas of life, fear is the absolute biggest barrier between where you are and where you want to be. Fear can literally stop you from living the life you desire.

It's the same thing in Marketing. Fear can hold you back from the success you deserve. The Troll personifies fears that are connected to the marketing of yourself and your work.

For most writers and artists, these fears are some kind of monstrous mix about who you really are, who you think you should be, what you need to say about your work, how much valuable time you have to 'waste' on marketing, how to overcome shyness or modesty to do social media, and, for many of us, how not to press the wrong button and accidentally share the wrong things with everyone on the Internet.

Somehow these common fears transform themselves figuratively into one monstrous troll that keeps you apart from your audience.

So, is there something you can do about the troll!?

Step Two:

Confront the Troll

Be brave!
Face your fears.

Step Three:

Conquer the Troll

Don't let the troll keep you apart from your dreams...or separate you from your audience.

As a writer or artist, your imagination will play a key role in how you handle the troll. This is an important concept to understand and use.

Because you are a creative individual, your imagination is naturally bigger-than-life. That means you have the capacity to almost always imagine a bigger troll than you will ever actually encounter under any bridge. Knowing the truth about your not-as-bad-as-you-imagined fears will help you find the courage to face your fears, whatever they are. If you take time to understand your fears, you can proactively do something to conquer the troll...and ultimately build the career you deserve.

Fear can really harm your creative career. For a writer or an artist, fear morphs quickly into worry, and worry in the creative realm can only be classified as mismanagement of your imagination. It helps to make it a rule that you won't waste your valuable creative energy spinning pointlessly in 'worry' mode. Worrying drains you. Worrying will negatively impact your creative productivity. Luckily, your imagination is trainable. The opposite of worrying is anticipating. Good things happen when you practice imagining the possibilities. So begin to proactively anticipate good things. Practice restricting yourself from imagining bad things. Do not allow fear to turn into a worryfest. Redirecting your imagination will make life much happier and your career opportunities will become much clearer. That action increases productivity. In turn, productivity feeds your creative spirit. And, that is what triumphs over the troll.

FRANK: I want to use the Internet but I don't feel like I know what to do with Facebook, Pinterest, Twitter, Tumblr, LinkedIn, Instagram, and all the other social media platforms.

ROBIN: Are you afraid of learning new things? Or is it something else?

FRANK: Well, technical things can feel overwhelming sometimes, but that isn't really the fear that bothers me the most. Secretly, I have a different fear that is a little hard to articulate. I think it boils down to the idea that I'm afraid once I actually get all my marketing plans going, it will take even more time to keep it all going—I don't want social media to take over my life!

ROBIN: So, you are afraid that if people find out about you that you will be obligated to interact. You are afraid of the time required for marketing yourself and your work?

FRANK: I don't want social media activities to steal precious time away from my art. I'm very afraid that I will lose all my creative time. I don't want to spend hours and hours each week talking to people when in my heart, I know that I would just rather spend that time drawing and creating my art…even if choosing to do that ultimately means less people will ever see my artwork.

ROBIN: You are not wrong to fear losing control of your creative time. I don't want that to happen to you. But this is not an "either/or" situation. You can safeguard your creative time and still effectively market yourself and your work. Inviting people to your Creative Castle is not giving them free reign of every room or offering them endless time. Safeguard your creative time. It is your Castle. You have the right to make sure your rules suit your most important needs. When it comes to social media, pick and choose. You don't have to do everything. So don't sabotage your future because of this fear.

Common Fears of Artists and Writers	Common Questions Artists and Writers Ask When They Are Afraid	What To Do...
The fear about who you are	Am I good enough? Will they like me?	Be clear. Be honest. Be real. Those qualities help people understand that you are indeed good enough.
The fear about what you say	Will I look stupid? Will I say the wrong thing? Will I look dumb trying?	Be kind. Be friendly. Be interested. These three qualities always outshine and outnumber anything that you do that could possibly appear stupid. Really.
The fear about time	Am I wasting my time doing the wrong things?	Everything you do takes more time than you want it to take. To avoid wasting time, set measurable goals. Find help when needed. Reserve and protect creative time so that you can always continue to create.
The fear about social media	Do I have to learn how to do it all? Can I learn how to do any of it? How do I even start?	Start slow. Take a cursory look at the different platforms and how they work. Pick one or two and let the others go. Linkedin is frequently good for business connections like agents, editors, museum curators, and librarians. Twitter is often frequented by media. Pinterest is a natural for artists. Good Reads is populated by readers. FineArtAmerica is filled with art lovers and fans who purchase art. Choose a platform that you like and one that you think a portion of your audience might like. Give one or two platforms a real try.

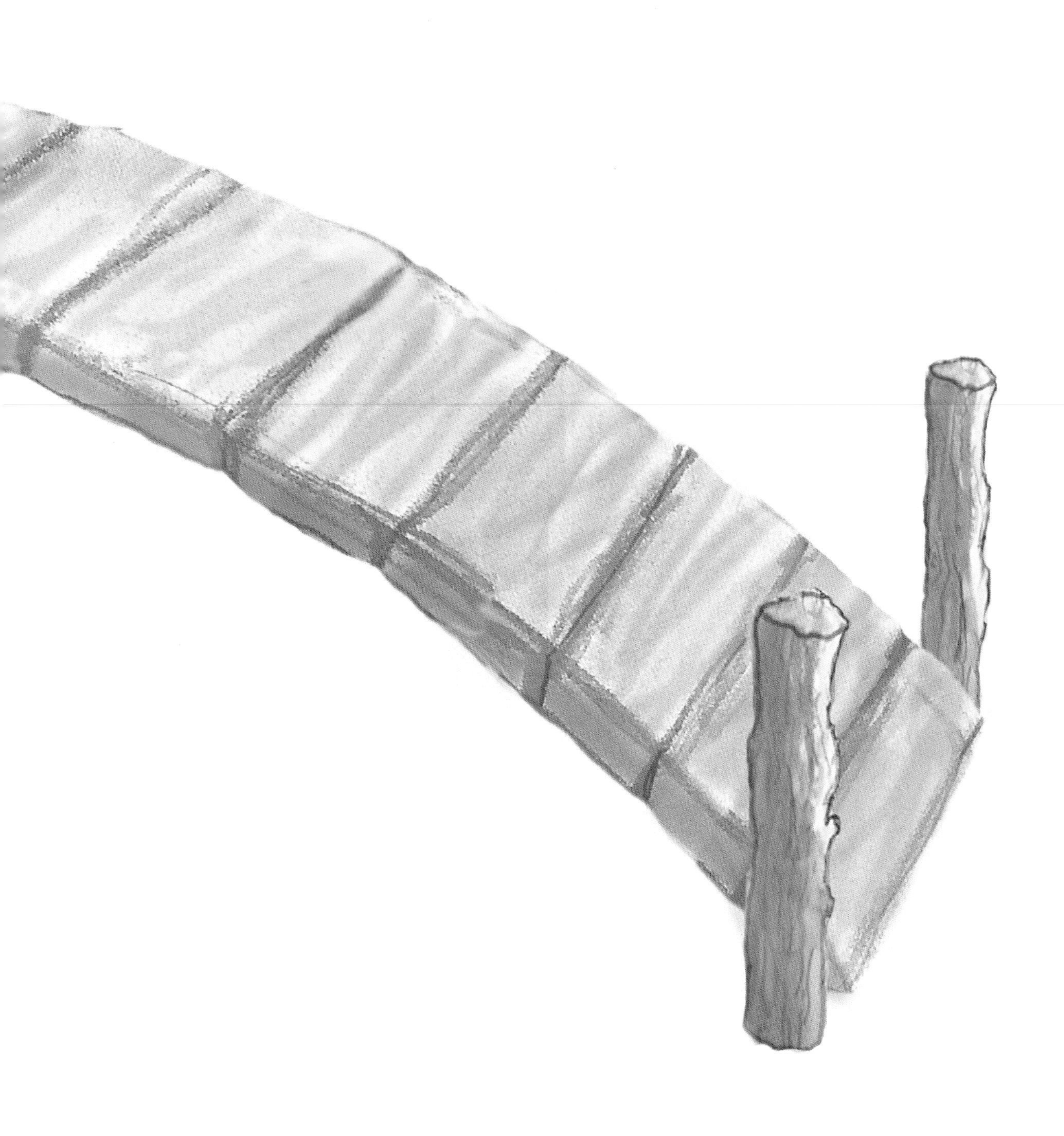

Chapter 5

The Bridge

It is not just the troll that can keep your audience from connecting with you.

The bridge itself can be a big barrier all its own. Both sides of the troll bridge need to be clear of obstacles. The closer fans get to you, the more difficult the journey typically becomes for them.

It's important to make every step of your fan's journey as easy as you can make it.

Start by taking a fresh, clear look at your bridge.

The world's first impression of you really matters. So, take a long, hard look at how people initially see you. Like many artists and writers, you may have gotten so busy focusing on your creative work that you stopped thinking about what your potential fans truly experience when they first encounter you.

Disregarding your public image is like neglecting the road-side portion of the bridge in front of your creative castle.

How you introduce yourself may need attention. How you describe your work may need to be repaired. Left neglected, people may hurry past this all-important connection point before you ever have a chance to interact with them.

You can do better than this. You must.

Ask yourself: "What do strangers think when they first encounter me? How do they feel?"

Look at what they see. Do you appear spectacular, amazing, and professional or unfriendly, amateur, and ordinary?

Do they think: 'I want to know this person'… or 'I wonder if this creative person is still actively working or has quit?'

CASTLE of
ARTIST
NO TRESPASSING!

Make Your Bridge and Your Gate More Welcoming.

The entire bridge—not just the roadside portion–is critical. You must make sure the connection path is warm and inviting. It must be wide open, not blocked. Few people will consider crossing a bridge that delivers them directly to a sinister-looking, locked gate. So make sure you are friendly and inviting.

In real life, your troll bridge encompasses everything from your business card to your website, social media platforms, newsletters, blogs, and all the other ways that connect you with your fans.

So, think about the first impression and the second one too. These days, it's important to realize that even if the world's first glimpse of you is in person, the second impression of you and your work will surely be a digital one. People will check you out online from their computers, tablets, and smart phones. Think hard how to deliberately build and maintain your online image.

Welcome to the Castle!
CASTLE of
ARTIST

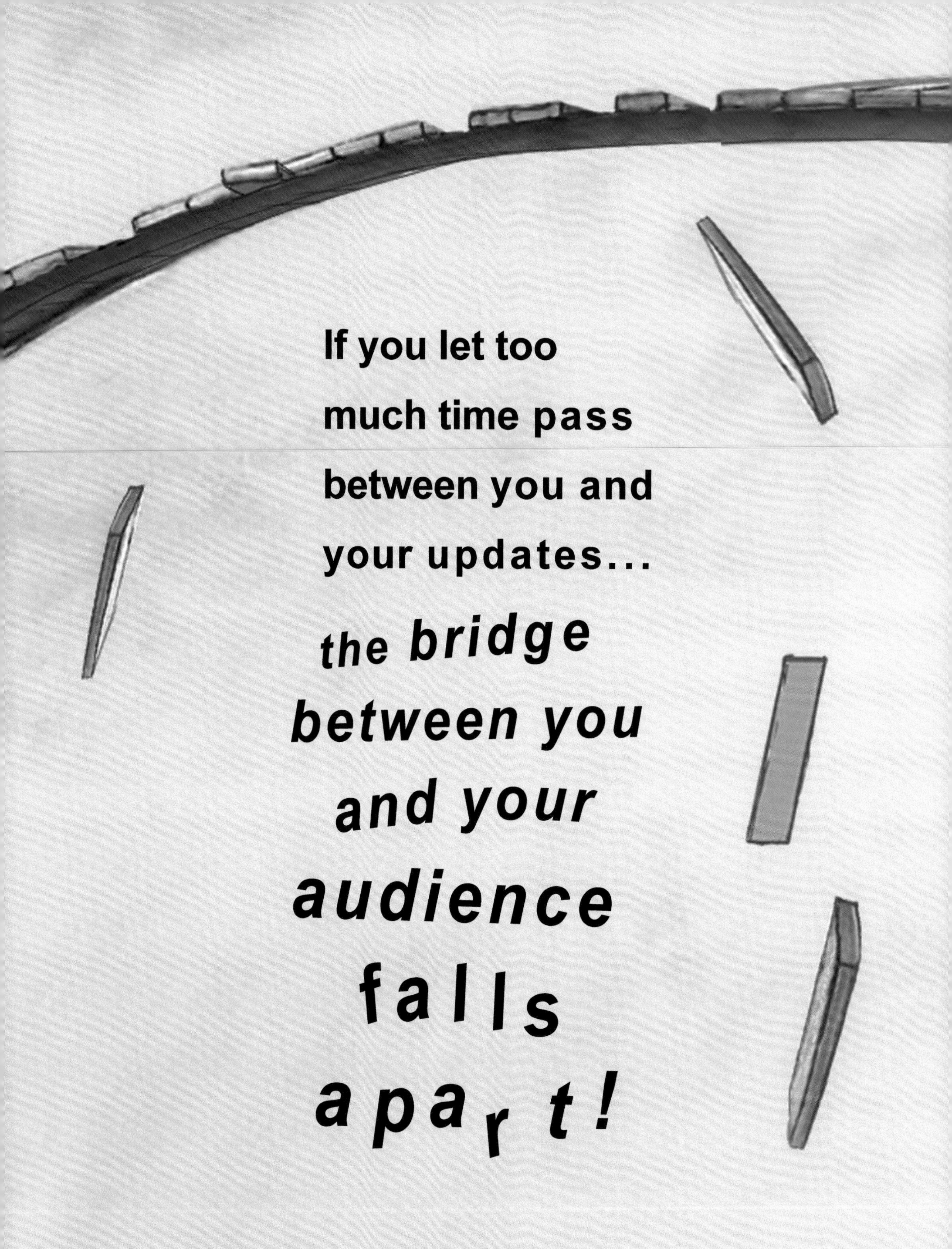
If you let too much time pass between you and your updates...
the bridge between you and your audience falls apart!

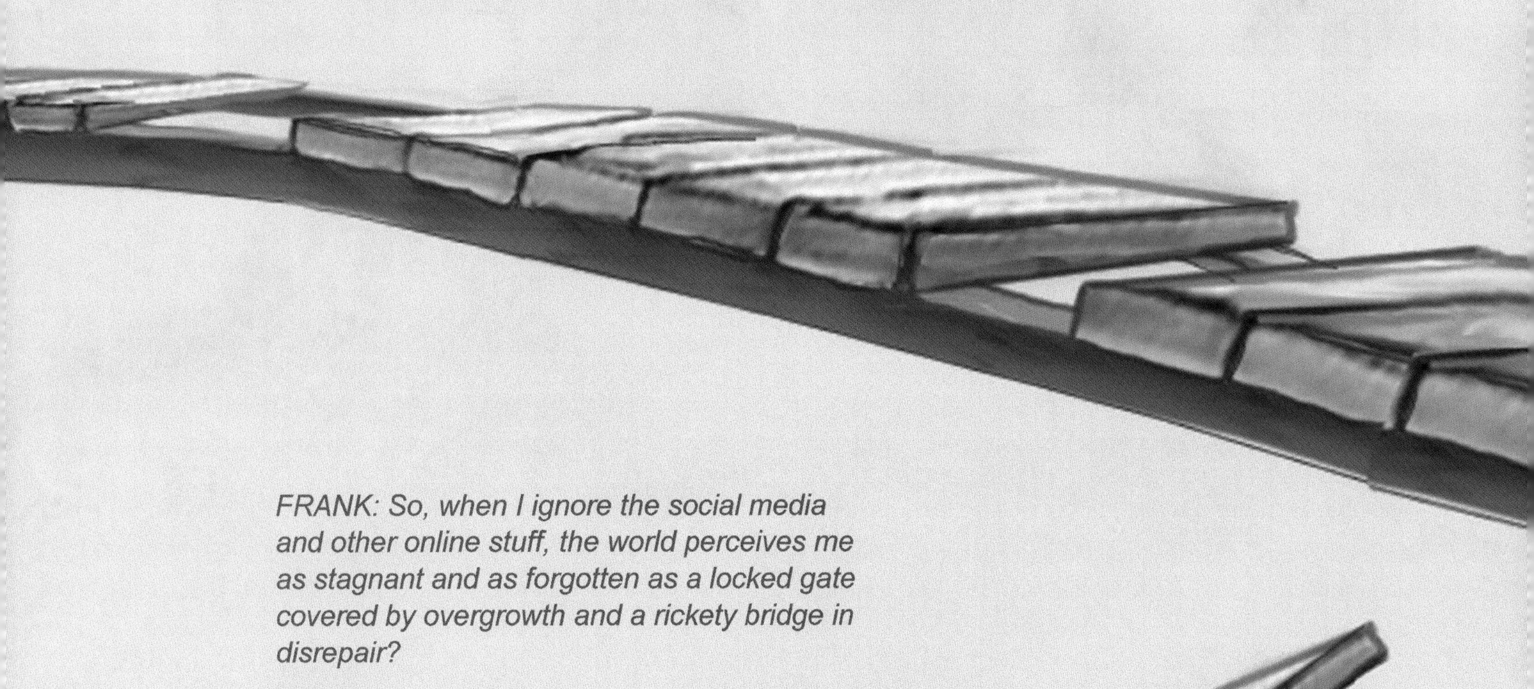

FRANK: So, when I ignore the social media and other online stuff, the world perceives me as stagnant and as forgotten as a locked gate covered by overgrowth and a rickety bridge in disrepair?

ROBIN: Yes. Realizing that your image may appear dull, confusing, really outdated or just plain wrong is often a bit of a shock. Your current profile descriptions may be so mysterious and conflicting that your desired audience cannot possibly decipher who you really are. Take a close look at what the public sees. Maybe you've unwittingly created a network of social media profiles that lack critical info and are sadly misrepresenting you and your current work to the world-at-large.

FRANK: I can see how conflicting messages could be scary to my audience…and I know trying to reach out to my audience can be scary to me.

ROBIN: Your online image should not appear outdated and forgotten. Your public identity, your image, your brand may need a swift makeover to generate the clarity and meaning needed by the people you want to be noticed and surrounded by. Like most creatives, you may have significantly changed, improved, or hit your professional stride since the last snapshot of who you are was shared online.

FRANK: What should I do?

ROBIN: Spruce things up. You don't want to scare people away by projecting the wrong impression.

You can safeguard your creative time and still effectively market yourself and your work.

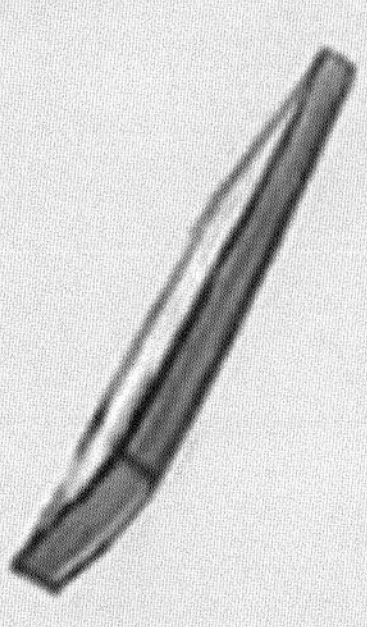

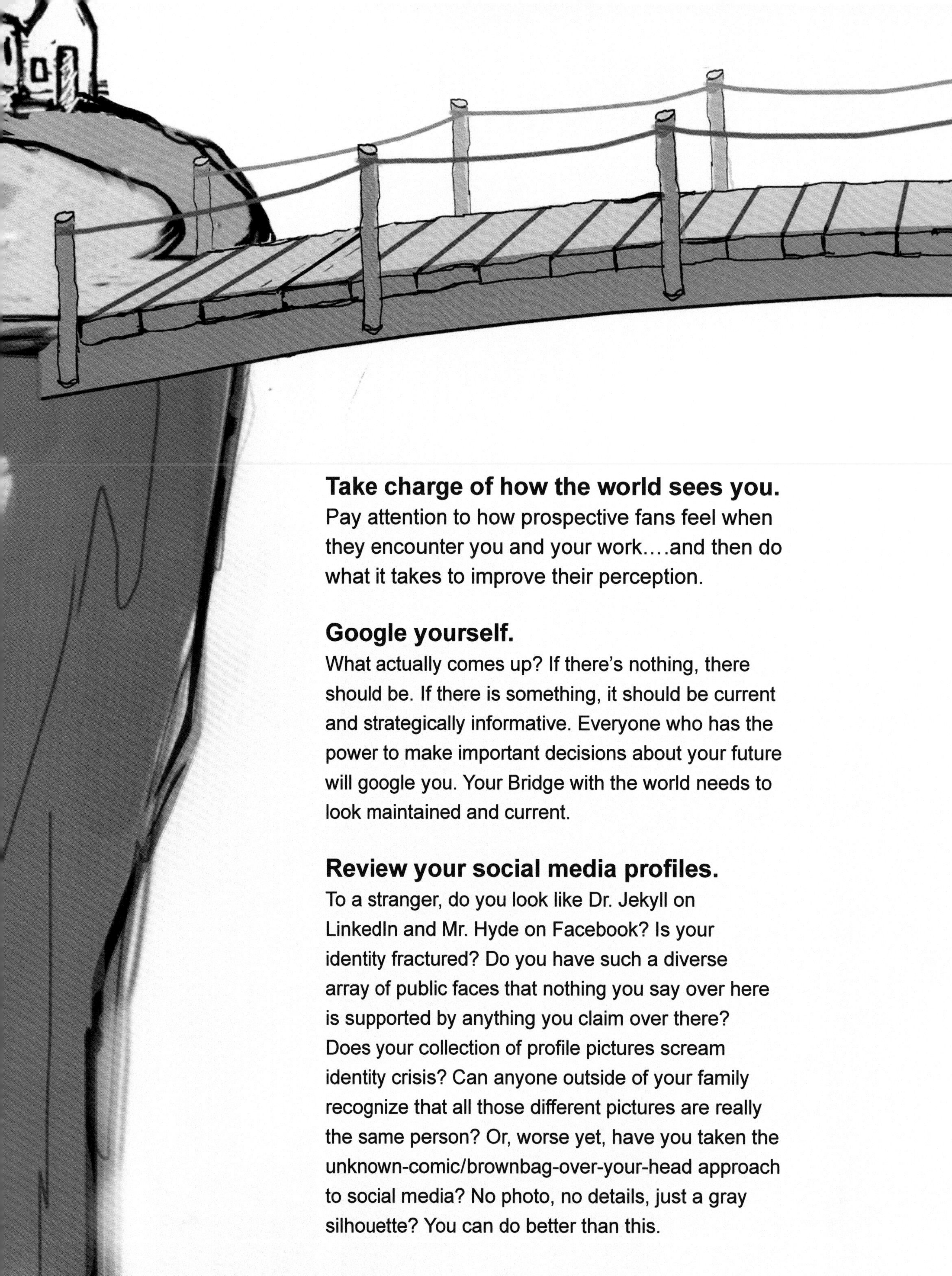

Take charge of how the world sees you.

Pay attention to how prospective fans feel when they encounter you and your work....and then do what it takes to improve their perception.

Google yourself.

What actually comes up? If there's nothing, there should be. If there is something, it should be current and strategically informative. Everyone who has the power to make important decisions about your future will google you. Your Bridge with the world needs to look maintained and current.

Review your social media profiles.

To a stranger, do you look like Dr. Jekyll on LinkedIn and Mr. Hyde on Facebook? Is your identity fractured? Do you have such a diverse array of public faces that nothing you say over here is supported by anything you claim over there? Does your collection of profile pictures scream identity crisis? Can anyone outside of your family recognize that all those different pictures are really the same person? Or, worse yet, have you taken the unknown-comic/brownbag-over-your-head approach to social media? No photo, no details, just a gray silhouette? You can do better than this.

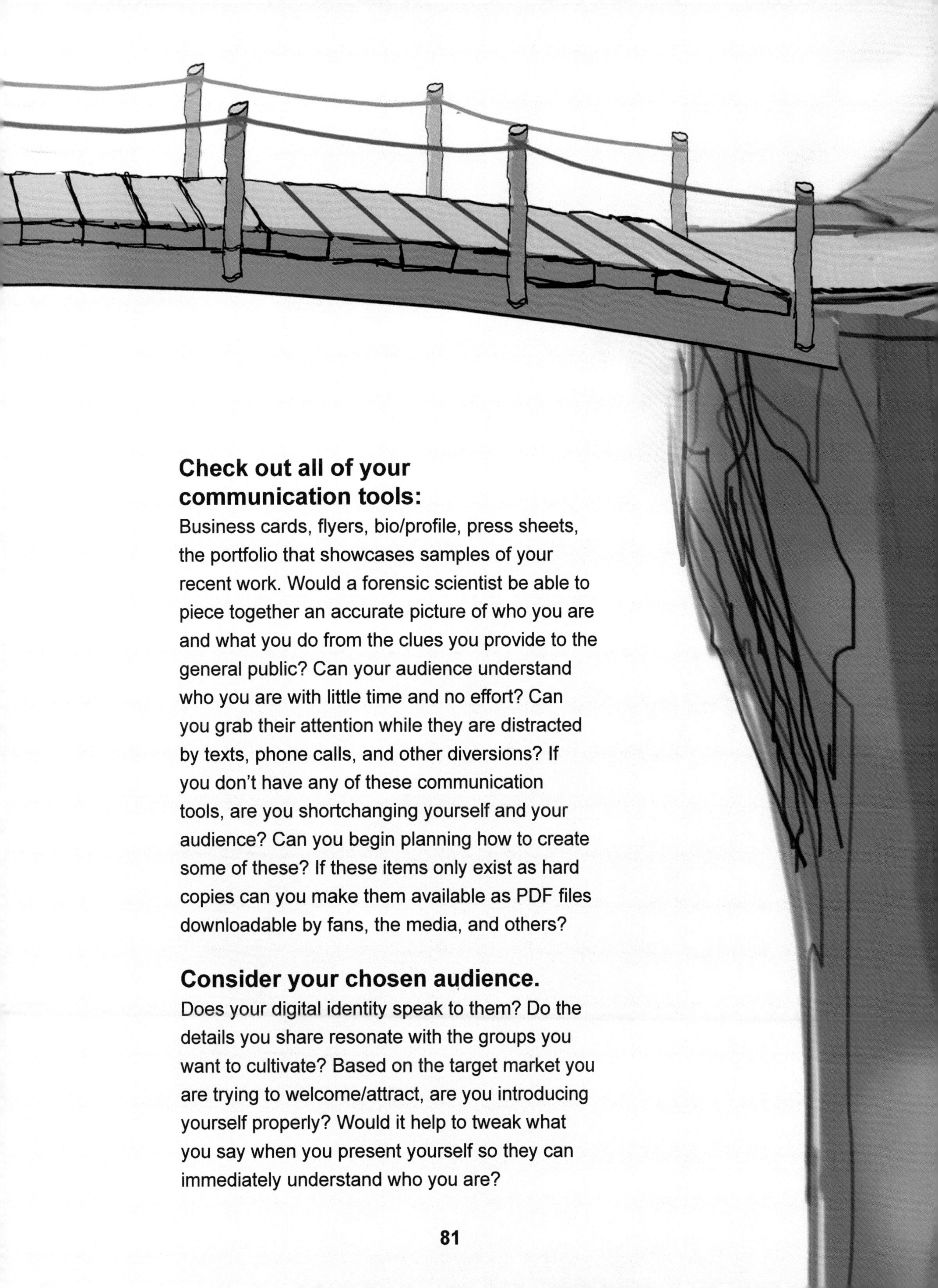

Check out all of your communication tools:

Business cards, flyers, bio/profile, press sheets, the portfolio that showcases samples of your recent work. Would a forensic scientist be able to piece together an accurate picture of who you are and what you do from the clues you provide to the general public? Can your audience understand who you are with little time and no effort? Can you grab their attention while they are distracted by texts, phone calls, and other diversions? If you don't have any of these communication tools, are you shortchanging yourself and your audience? Can you begin planning how to create some of these? If these items only exist as hard copies can you make them available as PDF files downloadable by fans, the media, and others?

Consider your chosen audience.

Does your digital identity speak to them? Do the details you share resonate with the groups you want to cultivate? Based on the target market you are trying to welcome/attract, are you introducing yourself properly? Would it help to tweak what you say when you present yourself so they can immediately understand who you are?

The Audience's Journey from the village to the castle...

	WHAT YOUR AUDIENCE NEEDS TO EXPERIENCE	WHAT YOU NEED TO DO FOR YOUR AUDIENCE
1. The Village	Your audience needs to discover you, become aware of you, and begin to recognize that you have creative treasures that they will love.	You need to make a focused effort to raise public awareness about who you are and what you do. Make sure that your online identity is current and up to date.
2. The Road 3. The Bridge	Your audience needs to find an easy way to connect with you and to find out more about you. Your audience needs to feel like an initial connection with you is leading to a deeper way to actively engage with you… for example, if they sign up for a newsletter, you need to send newsletters regularly. Or, if they reach out to you through social media, you need to make sure that you acknowledge them.	You need to make sure that when people become aware of you that it is easy for them to connect with you through email or on social media. Make sure it is easy for them to become part of your contacts such as a subscriber to your e-blasts or e-newsletters. Make sure you are ready to begin building a relationship with them by adding their name and contact info to your database.
4. The Troll	Your audience should see no evidence of trolls.	Make sure that your public identity is welcoming and friendly, not troll-like.
5. The Gate	Entry to your kingdom should be welcoming, exciting, and easy.	You need to remove anything that is distracting and outdated. Make sure work samples are viewable online.

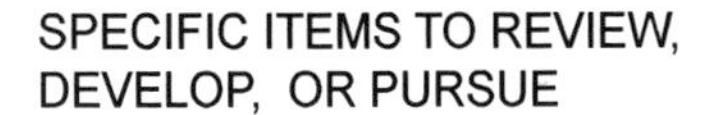

SPECIFIC ITEMS TO REVIEW, DEVELOP, OR PURSUE

- Your Website
- Your Social Media Profiles
- Youtube
- Articles About You
- Events that Feature You
- Ads Selling Your Work
- Newsletter Articles
- Blog Articles

- Create buttons (links) on your website to help visitors connect with you on Facebook or any of your preferred social media platforms. At the bottom of your emails add a "standard signature line" in your outgoing emails that encourage people to call you, visit your website, or connect with you on your preferred social media platform.
- Traditional business cards
- Database that organizes and categorizes all of your contacts

- Social Media Profiles must not conflict with each other. The same photo of you can create unity between platforms.

- Your Website
- Your Social Media Profiles
- Online Portfolio or Gallery
- Blog Articles
- Downloadable Press Kit

You are almost all set! But you still have a few things left to do before your fans arrive. One of the most important parts of the entire marketing adventure is immediately ahead...The Doors!

Get Ready.

People notice when you make

things appear more inviting.

Your Audience is likely already headed your way.

You don't have to let the internet and social media take over your life! Build a bridge between you and your audience that actually supports your creative life. You can choose to create a bridge that gives you an adequate amount of time for dreaming and creating.

You can control the situation.
Build the Bridge YOU Choose.

Chapter 6

The Doors

As an artist or writer, you're already familiar with the critical part of the creative process that's all about crafting the end of your project. When it comes to your creative work, you are willing to spend hours and hours considering exactly how to wrap up the hero's journey or how to ultimately deliver the final visual punch you've been imagining in your mind's eye.

You may not have realized that your marketing strategy requires that same sort of creative focus as a story or drawing.

The business side of your creativity will take off when the power of your imagination is applied to it. We've found that writers and artists can transform their own careers when we help them see the 'ending' part of their marketing adventure in a new way.

Metaphorically, a special set of doors inside your Creative Castle's Grand Meeting Room will help you understand how to unlock your imagination and approach that ending differently.

So, let's transform your creative career forever. Let's check out The Doors.

The Doors are strategically located in The Grand Meeting Room.

Like any great story or painting, the setting for these Doors truly matters. This is the same room where previously you spent so much time making the display tables look amazing for each niche of your audience.

Imagine this. The Grand Meeting Room is all decked out with your creative treasures.

The whole marketing adventure is about sharing your creative treasures with people who have the capacity to care about your work. Castle visitors need to know who you truly are and what your work is all about. This is the place where you can answer their questions and help them discover the importance of your products and services. Your work is meant to inspire or educate or entertain them. You will motivate them or bring them joy or provide understanding in a million different ways.

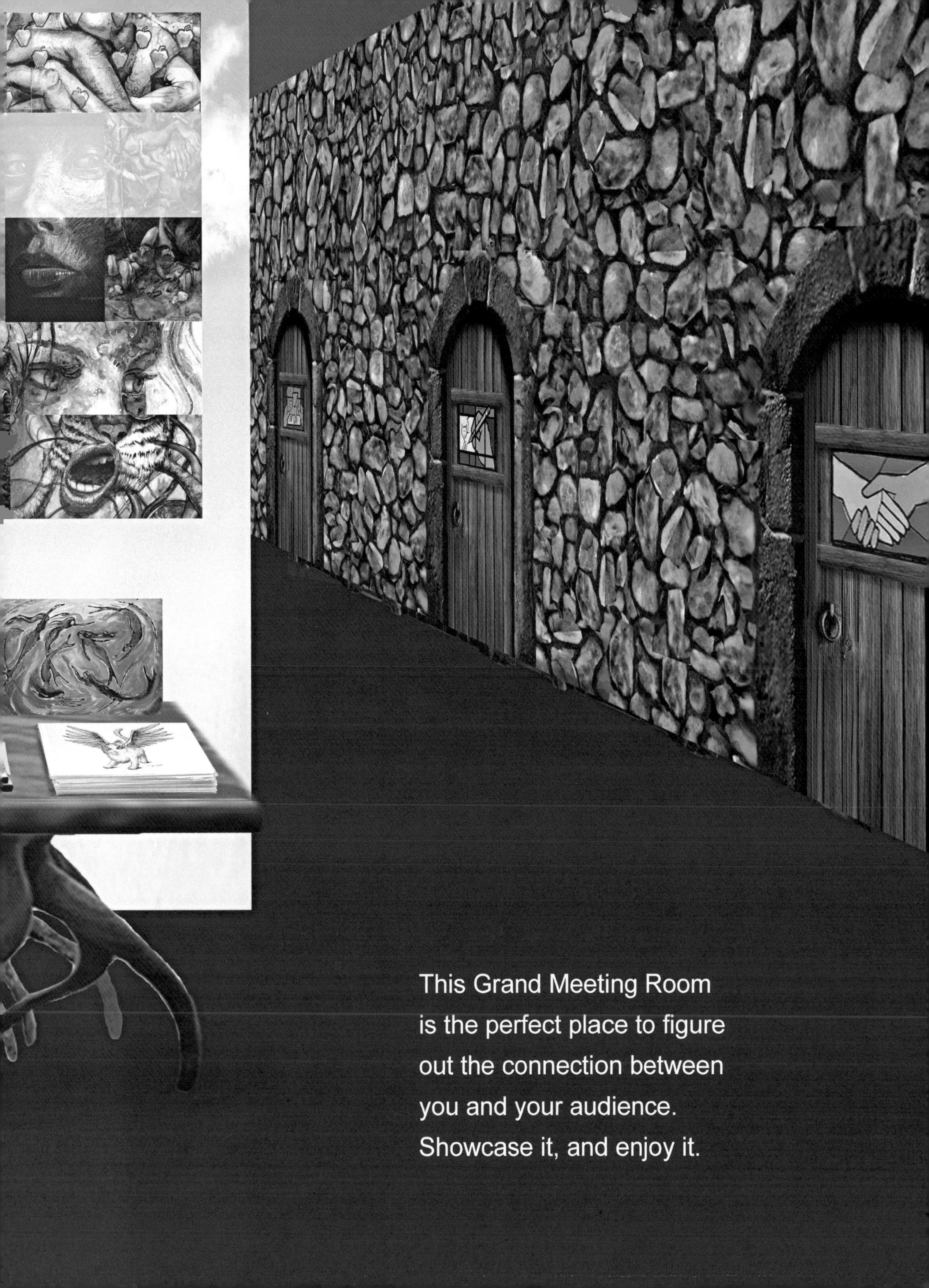
This Grand Meeting Room
is the perfect place to figure
out the connection between
you and your audience.
Showcase it, and enjoy it.

You have built four fabulous displays to intrigue and delight each of your audience groups.

There is so much to see. Each table highlights a key aspect of your work for your audience to focus upon and enjoy. The four display tables exude your brand. Every detail in the room purposefully speaks loudly of who you are and what you do. When visitors arrive here, they can breathe you in and clearly understand what you and your work are truly about.

Artists Learning to Draw

Young Fantasy Art Lovers

The idea of breathing in your brand can feel overwhelming if you are not sure what your brand actually is yet. However, when you focus on designing this room, articulating your brand is what naturally happens. Choosing your work carefully for the four tables will help you convey the unique aspects and facets of your brand...whatever stage you are currently at in the development of that brand.

The Art Gallery Crowd

Creatives Struggling with Depression

Finally, and most importantly, you must understand the Significance of The Doors.

So far, we've focused on bringing people to the room. But, equally important is the manner in which you plan for them to leave. When it's time for guests to leave the Grand Meeting Room, you must help them find the appropriate door to use as an exit. Each Door accommodates a different top desire that is commonly expressed by audience members.

After experiencing your creative treasures, most people typically want one of three things:

1. **to buy a product from you**
2. **to purchase a service (hire you to do something)**
3. **to remember the experience and tell a friend**

Make sure each option can happen for your audience...and for you!

Many artists and writers don't realize that The Doors are the most essential part of marketing. The success of your creative career is literally hinged on understanding these three doors. So, take the time to take time to explore and utilize this important strategy.

Here's what you need to know...After your audience has become acquainted with you and your work, you must be a good host and help them take the next logical step. Do not shortchange your fans...guide them to the door they most desire.

Visualizing these three doors can help you raise awareness for yourself and your work...and can help you make a better income from your creative career.

FRANK: I want my career to last…and I want it to be profitable.

ROBIN: For most creatives, understanding the final stage of marketing can make a huge difference. You wouldn't consider a book to be complete without an ending. Right? You wouldn't stop in the middle of a painting and feel like it was done. Marketing has an ending, too.

FRANK: What does the ending look like?

ROBIN: It's important to know that both creating an on-going relationship with your fans and making a solid income are the natural outcomes of your marketing adventure. When you carefully prepare the journey for your fans they will have a fun experience, and many fans will then be interested in buying a product or service from you.

Door #1

The Products Door

This door opens to your own little gift shop where items you've created are available for purchase. These items are completely finished. If you're an author, the products might be copies of your book, workbook, e-book, or audio book. If you're an artist, the products might be just your original creations. But you could also consider including reproductions of your artwork. You might decide to include novelty items that feature your artwork– like phone covers, mugs, key-chains, jigsaw puzzles, playing cards, T-Shirts, skateboards, and an endless array of other fun accessories.

Four Things to Know:

- Make sure you have finished products to sell. For some creative people it is easy to start creative work and it's hard to finish it. You can't sell unfinished work.

- Your products need to be tagged with prices. Imagine going into a store that had no price tags...don't do that. Price your items.

- Figure out a way to do commerce. Imagine a store with no cash register...don't stop a sale because you can't accept a credit card. Even smart phones can take credit cards...Look into it.

- Think about who your buyer is when you create products. The more products that are geared to the same type of buyer, the better. It is easier to sell three items to the same person than the same item to three different people. In fact, when you have three items to sell to the same buyer, things will change for you in a very good way.

Door #2

The Service Door

This door opens to a special chamber where a prospective customer can talk to you about hiring you for services that you are willing to perform. If you are a writer, someone might wonder if you are available to write or edit special projects like feature articles, memoirs, video scripts, promotional collateral, radio advertisements, and more. If you are an artist, someone might wonder about commissioning you to create a portrait, design a book cover, create an ad graphic, create a book illustration, do a set design, design a product, or more.

Four Things to Know:

- Make sure you request a fair price for your work as a creative contractor and strongly consider asking for at least a portion of your payment up front. The problem with creative work is that if someone fails to pay you, you cannot get back the time you invested.

- Get details in writing. Service agreements can help you visualize the process more clearly. Managing expectations will help you and your customer.

- Figure out a way to do commerce. You may need to create an agreement, an invoice, and a receipt. And you will need a way to accept payment.

- Create a rate card. Even if you do not publicly share your rate card, build one for yourself to use. Do the math and double-check it so that you can quote hourly rates or flat rates for projects without robbing yourself.

Door #3
The Meet-And-Greet Door

This door leads to a place that is as important as the first two doors. This exit is for guests who don't want to buy a product and who don't want to buy a service...at least, not yet. (And truthfully, maybe never–and that is OK.) For now, many of your fans will only enjoy what you do. In the future, some of these fans will choose to buy something or hire you. Fans can deeply love your work and still not have the funds to buy it, or the place to keep it, or the ability to make it part of their lives. You cannot control whether someone buys a product or service from you, but you can control your response to their choice. Choose to show gratitude and thank your guests for visiting your creative castle. Provide a token of appreciation to help them remember you and your work. This token can enable them to make meaningful referrals to people they know who might like what you do.

A token of appreciation can come in a variety of formats. Offering a free gift or helpful info presents a good opportunity to obtain the email address of your fans which can help you continue to build relationships with them.

Tips on Giveaways:

- In person, you should give away things like a business card, brochure, or some other item for them to remember you by.

- For giveaways on the internet, select a free product people will love: an e-book, a print of your art, a link to something of value, or whatever amazing thing you think of. Always capture their email address in exchange for a give away.

- You can search on the internet for more cool ideas about giveaways.

The Light of Your Creativity

Can Shine From Every Part of Who You Are...

Not Just From Your Work, but Also From Your Marketing Tactics.

Make it easy for people to see who you are.

It starts with clear written messages and memorable illustrations. Keep things clear and on-point.

Double check:

- Your website navigation
- Your social media profiles
- Articles about you
- Events that feature you
- Flyers
- Ads selling your work
- Blog posts written by you
- Messages that have special meaning to each of your four chosen groups
- Make buying stuff smooth and hassle-free.

Your audience needs to understand what they can buy.

To sell products, you need to have finished items that can actually be purchased immediately. Consider ways to maximize each piece you have created. For example, a book might be available as an e-book, an audio book, and a traditional paperback. A piece of art might be available as a poster or as a customized phone case.

Double check:

- Prices
- Buy now buttons
- Devices for your phone or tablet to swipe credit cards

Make hiring you simple and straightforward.

Your audience needs to understand the parameters of your work as a creative contractor. You need to articulate the services you are willing to perform. Be specific.

Double check:

- Service agreements
- Invoice templates
- Rate card (even if you do not publicly share your rate card, build one for yourself to use.)

Make it easy to come back or refer a friend.

Double check:

- Connection buttons to your social media
- Sign-up forms for newsletters or e-blasts
- Business cards
- Brochures
- Downloadable catalogs
- Downloadable press kits
- Coupon

Chapter 7

The Adventure

The whole marketing adventure is simply about sharing your creative treasures with people who care about your work.

Your fans are out there, and they would love to find you. But it's really up to you to make this possible.

So come on! Your journey awaits. This amazing adventure can make your life—and the lives of others around the world—happier, richer, and fuller.

But is marketing really that simple?

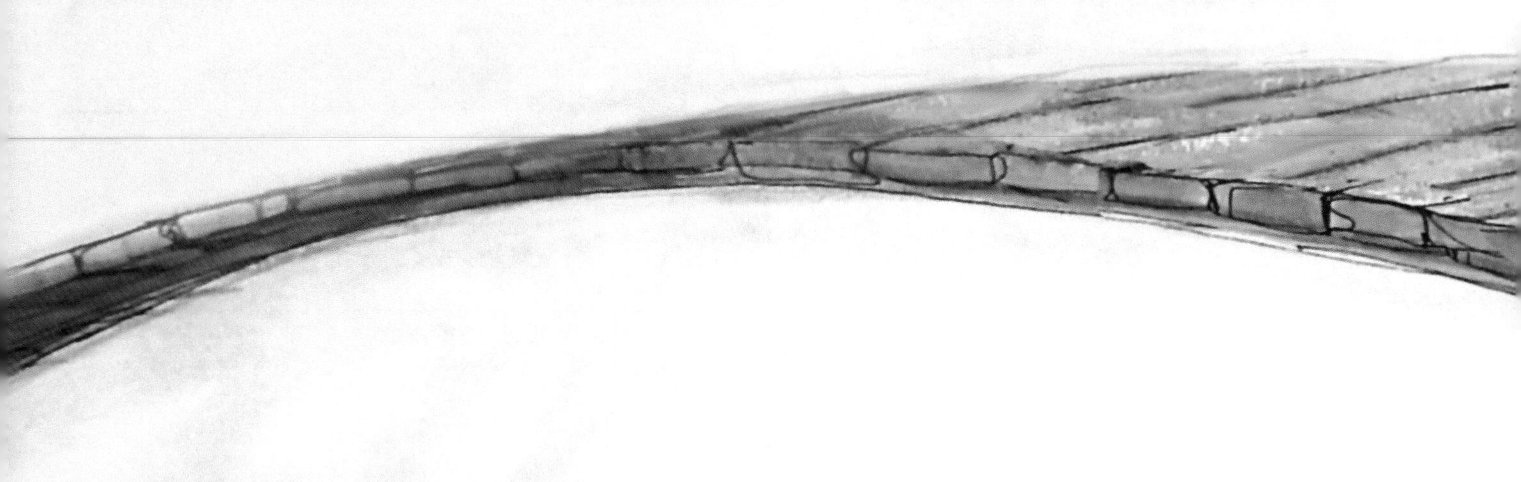

Yes, it's that simple.

When you make it possible
for you and your audience to
c o n n e c t, like magic,
more and more bridges will appear!

12 Steps to Succeed in the Adventure
of Marketing Yourself and Your Creative Work

1. **Take Time.** Invest the necessary time in your "creative castle" (months or years) to build up your skills so that what you create is of high quality.

2. **Finish your work.** Before you market, you need quality products you can display and sell.

3. **Clearly identify your audience.** Use your "telescope" to find 4 special groups who will love what you do.

4. **Examine the path.** Do your fans have to cross a rickety bridge with a troll under it to get to you? Is the gate to your castle open or locked?

5. **Fix your troll bridge.** Spend the time necessary so that your fans can easily find you and get to you. Your "bridge" includes all the ways your audience can connect with you. (It could include your website, Facebook page, blog, a store front, websites where you sell your work, trade shows, arts and crafts festivals, emails, and more.)

6. **Face your fears.** Take charge over the troll (your fears and your audience's fears) so these fears don't stop you from becoming successful.

7. **Focus on the fun.** Marketing is a natural extension of your creativity. Have fun spending some time making the complete journey a wonderful experience for your fans…fun to cross the bridge, fun to pass through your castle gate, fun to enter your castle, and fun to make it all the way to your Grand Meeting Room.

8. **Showcase your work.** Take the time needed to masterfully display your creations so that your fans have a great time looking at your work.

9. **Unlock the Doors.** Create the engagement strategy for your fans, customers, and your entire audience. These 3 doors– the Product Door, the Service Door, and the Meet-and-Greet Door– are very important, because this is how you actually promote yourself and eventually make money.

10. **Live the Adventure!** Find a way…or create one. Remember that this is your adventure, your creative castle. You can choose the amount of space and time you spend creating and the amount of space and time you devote to marketing. You can decide exactly what is right for you.

11. **Maintain the Path.** After you have spent time to create your products, find your audience, fix the bridge for your audience to cross, and create your tables and exits in your Grand Meeting Room– you need to remember to monitor all these things and keep them in good working order over the coming months and years.

12. **Enjoy.** Celebrate that you are successfully marketing yourself and that your audience is crossing the troll bridge and connecting with you!! **You are doing it!**

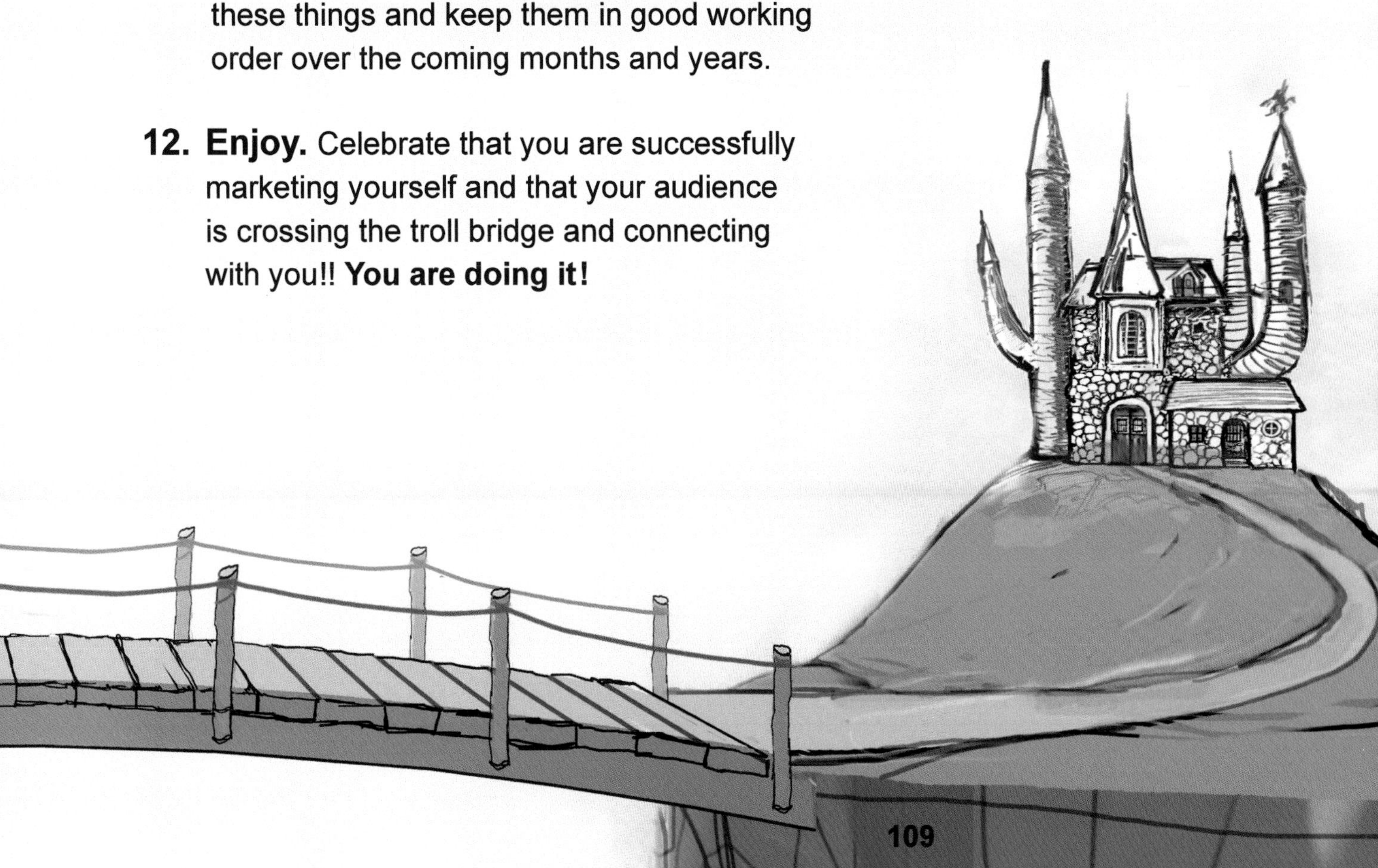

I REMEMBER WHEN I WAS 14 YEARS OLD GOING DOOR-TO-DOOR TRYING TO GET PEOPLE TO BUY A SUBSCRIPTION TO A NEWSPAPER. I STILL REMEMBER NOT LIKING THE EXPERIENCE OF PEOPLE BARELY OPENING THE DOOR WHILE I TRIED TO CONVINCE THEM TO BUY SOMETHING.

I THINK I HAVE ALWAYS THOUGHT THAT WAS THE WAY MARKETING HAD TO BE: I WOULD HAVE TO LEAVE MY "CREATIVITY CASTLE," CROSS THE "SCARY BRIDGE," AND GO KNOCK ON THE DOORS AT THE "VILLAGE" TRYING TO FIND PEOPLE WHO WOULD BUY MY ART.

BUT I HAVE NEVER WANTED TO BE A "PUSHY SALESMAN"! SO MOST OF MY ADULT LIFE I HAVE NOT DONE VERY WELL AT MARKETING MYSELF...

BUT THIS BOOK HAS CATAPULTED ME
TO A NEW TRUTH, THAT, AS A
CREATIVE ARTIST,
I REALLY LIKE:

I DON'T HAVE TO
GO TO THE VILLAGE
AND KNOCK ON DOORS.
INSTEAD, I JUST NEED TO
PREPARE THE WAY FOR
MY FANS TO COME TO ME!

SO, MARKETING CAN BE FUN.
I JUST NEED TO CREATE AN
"IRRESISTABLE PATH OF BREADCRUMBS"
(THINK OF THE HANSEL AND GRETEL STORY)
FOR MY AUDIENCE TO FOLLOW ACROSS THE BRIDGE,
THROUGH THE CASTLE GATE, INTO THE CASTLE
TO THE GRAND MEETING ROOM, AND EVENTUALLY
THROUGH ONE OF THE THREE EXIT DOORS.

AND THIS ENTIRE
BREADCRUMB TRAIL COULD
ALL BE ON THE INTERNET—

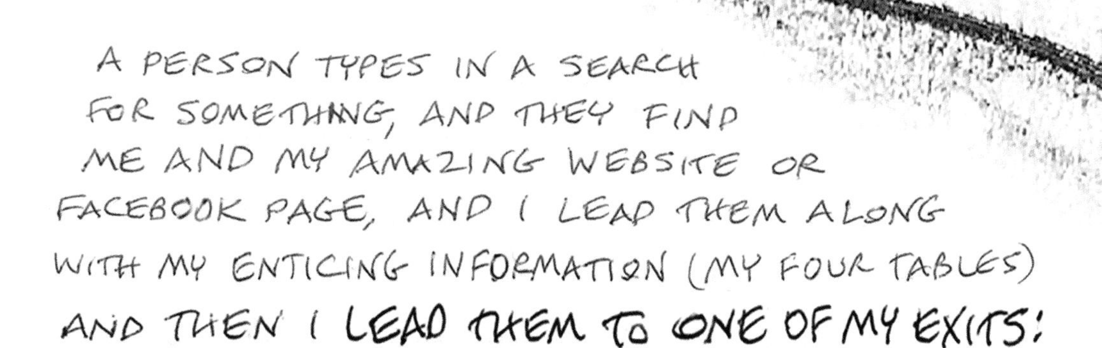

A PERSON TYPES IN A SEARCH FOR SOMETHING, AND THEY FIND ME AND MY AMAZING WEBSITE OR FACEBOOK PAGE, AND I LEAD THEM ALONG WITH MY ENTICING INFORMATION (MY FOUR TABLES) AND THEN I LEAD THEM TO ONE OF MY EXITS:

1. THEY BUY A PRODUCT
2. THEY BUY A SERVICE
3. THEY HAD A MEMORABLE FUN EXPERIENCE MEETING ME

IF I DESIGNED A FUN EXPERIENCE AT MY WEBSITE (OR BLOG, FACEBOOK PAGE ETC) THEY WILL LOOK FORWARD TO COMING BACK TO VISIT MANY MORE TIMES IN THE FUTURE.

WHEN I CREATE AN ENJOYABLE JOURNEY FOR MY AUDIENCE SOMETHING AMAZING HAPPENS— THE "TROLL" WILL MAGICALLY DISAPPEAR! WHEN YOU MAKE THE BRIDGE AN ENJOYABLE SAFE EXPERIENCE THE AUDIENCE HAS NOTHING TO FEEL NERVOUS ABOUT OR AFRAID OF!

NOW IT IS TIME FOR ME (AND YOU) TO START DOING THINGS I HAVE LEARNED ABOUT FROM THIS BOOK. I HAD FUN DRAWING THE PICTURES FOR THE 4 TABLES IN THE GRAND MEETING ROOM.

I ESPECIALLY LIKED THE PICTURE OF "LONG ARMS DRAWING FANTASY CREATURES" FOR MY "DRAWFANTASYCREATURES.COM" TABLE. AS I WRITE THESE WORDS I HAVE NOT YET FINISHED CREATING THIS WEBSITE OR THE BOOK! CREATING THE TABLES ACTUALLY GAVE ME SOME GREAT IDEAS FOR NEW PROJECTS I WANT TO CREATE OR FINISH CREATING.

I THINK YOU TOO WILL
ENJOY CREATING A PATH
FOR YOUR AUDIENCE TO
FIND YOU! IF YOU MAKE
THE AUDIENCE'S JOURNEY
FUN AND ENTERTAINING,
THEY WILL BE GLAD
THEY FOUND YOU—
AND JUST MAYBE,
THEY WON'T BE ABLE
TO RESIST BUYING
SOMETHING FROM YOU...
AND YOU ARE
FINALLY HAVING
FUN MARKETING
YOURSELF!!
Frank

Robin Blakely and Frank Robert Dixon are the creators of Crossing the Troll Bridge.

Robin is the CEO of Creative Center of America, a career coach, and the author of several business books. creativecenterofamerica.com

Frank is an award-winning artist, an art instructor, and the author of several art books. frankrobertdixon.com

We made this book to help creative people find a better more enjoyable way to market themselves and their creative works. If you would like additional help, inspiration, or creative support, visit **crossingthetrollbridge.com** for a variety of fear-less products and services designed to encourage and enlighten artists and writers.

To download your free 8"x10" motivational print (suitable for framing) of page 47: "Take Ownership of Your Creative Castle", go to **https://gumroad.com/l/uGqE**

CPSIA information can be obtained at www.ICGtesting.com
Printed in the USA
LVIW01n0827261216
518697LV00014B/66